# FROM THE ATTIC

## MONICA R. WICKS

INDIA • SINGAPORE • MALAYSIA

Copyright © Monica Wicks 2025
All Rights Reserved.

ISBN
Paperback 979-8-89632-350-1
Hardcase 979-8-89699-351-3

This book has been published with all efforts taken to make the material error-free after the consent of the author. However, the author and the publisher do not assume and hereby disclaim any liability to any party for any loss, damage, or disruption caused by errors or omissions, whether such errors or omissions result from negligence, accident, or any other cause.

While every effort has been made to avoid any mistake or omission, this publication is being sold on the condition and understanding that neither the author nor the publishers or printers would be liable in any manner to any person by reason of any mistake or omission in this publication or for any action taken or omitted to be taken or advice rendered or accepted on the basis of this work. For any defect in printing or binding the publishers will be liable only to replace the defective copy by another copy of this work then available.

# Dedication

To everyone who brought me experiences—
For the lessons, the growth, and the stories.
that found their way into these pages.

# Contents

## Section II:  A Mirror, Some Photographs, and Charms . . . 51

# *Preface*

This collection began with an attic—a metaphorical space where I tucked away forgotten moments, unresolved questions, and the bittersweet treasures of my past. Over time, I found myself drawn to it, uncovering not only what was stored there but what I needed to understand about myself.

Each section of this book reflects a stage of discovery:
- Cobwebs: The dusty, tangled memories we're hesitant to touch.
- A Mirror, Some Photographs, and Charms: The pieces that remind us of who we are, who we were, and the magic that lingers.
- A Light Through the Cracks and Some Keys: The hope and clarity that emerge when we finally unlock those hidden spaces.

These poems are my attic, and in opening it, I hope to inspire you to explore your own.

# Introduction

Some write with every beat of their heart, puncturing their veins to bleed on paper, hoping it will drain the sorrow out, while some write like flowers growing through concrete—

Words that need no nurturing, they just grow in them, no matter what.

Some write so their mind is a less crowded room, making space with every word they bring out. The power of the pen is within all of us, to stitch words together and cloak someone else with what they feel is what I aspire to do and motivate each one out there to just write, write from the heart, write from your attic.

Naming the book from the attic took a lot of consideration, an attic is more than a storage space—it's a time capsule, a quiet witness to the lives we've lived. "From the Attic" reflects this metaphor, inviting you to journey through its sections.

In Cobwebs, you'll encounter the neglected corners, where things feel heavy, tangled, and untouched. Moving through A Mirror, Some Photographs, and Charms, the perspective shifts as memories and symbols come into focus, offering clarity and connection. Finally, in A Light Through the Cracks and Some Keys, you'll discover the hope that filters through even the darkest spaces, illuminating a path forward.

This book is an exploration of rediscovery—a way of unearthing what's been buried and finding meaning in what remains.

I write to anyone who reads because if I am to use my voice,
I'm afraid I'll never stop screaming.

# SECTION I

## Cobwebs

# *Silhouettes*

I kept searching for your shadows fallen on the ground.
Collecting evidence of your existence.
Tugging the red thread and chasing silhouettes
to trace my being back to you.

# I pray for the angels

I pray for the angels,
with hands trembling,
knowing they, too,
bend under the weight of us.

Their wings, once mirrors of light,
are streaked with ash,
There is no measure for this ruin,
no tally to mark how far
we have let shadows stretch.

And so, I pray,
not for salvation,
but for their endurance.
For the edges of their feathers
not to fray into nothing.

I am sorry
for the prayers they bear,
for the weight of our sorrow,
and the cold distance
between us and the divine.

# *It was spring again*

When you left, I met new people.
saw words crumbling from their lips,
some affectionate, some boastful,
some tedious stories, others long anecdotes.

As I sat there watching words boomerang from my ears,
everything around grew dark,
they looked like skeletal remains.
with dead flowers falling from their jaws,
every time they moved it.
the flowers crumble and turn to dust.

A gentle breeze carried a whiff of a familiar cologne.
and snapped its fingers to throw me into the past,
dragging me to that afternoon.
where your shirt hugged my bare skin.
and I filled my lungs with your scent.

Curling up on the edge of your bed,
listening to you talk, it was spring again.

# Revolve

Your love is like a chilled shower.
trickling down my spine,
I gasp for breath while.
still getting used to it.
Resting my palm on your chest.
I try to make the earth revolve a little slower.

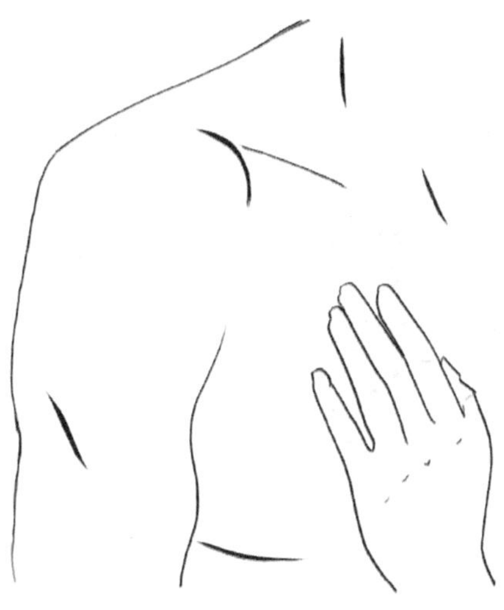

# Box of words, box of wounds?

Through the years, I met many words.
I kept trying to understand each of them.
learn, read between the lines.
Stored them, stacked them,
I piled them on my spine.
Hid them in boxes new.
I kept listening, I kept sinking,
with no anchor to rescue.

I revisited the box
every time I talked,
The pile kept rising.
Of all the words I stocked.

I saw the box one day,
bleed of dark red,
I touched and it hurt,
How? They were words heard and said.

I felt the ache rise in my spine.
Where I stored those that felt mine.
Little did I know they were not words but wounds.
Cut with a tear and sealed with a sign.

I asked them where they came from,
they said they were always here.
Collecting companions
who shared the same fear!

I sat there dumb,
saw the box bleed.
My mind went numb,
watch my heart's greed.

I collected wounds,
in the form of words.
And now I live in paralysis,
paralysis of those words.

# *I wait, somehow.*

Here comes the dawn again,
here comes my wait,
Light breaks, searing my gaze.
Like a burning grate.
I've stood here far too long,
from where you left to where I belong.
Shouldn't you be here by now?
My hope dissolves; I don't know how,
The sun has risen, yet I still wait somehow.

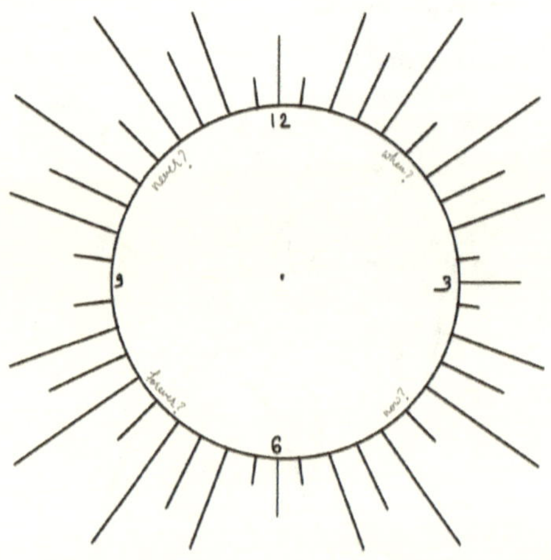

# *That is how my universe was left ajar.*

Shaky fingers with a cigarette in them;
ring finger adorned with a gem,
black nail polish that traps the night.
blurry eyes with no will to fight.
There's only glitter out,
shoes, dress, and on lips that pout.

 I saw him there,
blurred outline, a human nightmare
I saw him walk away,
as he found an empty stall,
"Who would want to live there?
with nothing everywhere?"
I saw his hands shine,
for he stole what was left of mine,
like dust, his fingernails carried my stars,
Just like that, is how my universe was left ajar.

# It's all still here.

The sea curls up to the shore,
I've watched the sand go.
and the sea comes back for more.
It's been so for years, I'm sure.
The sea is still here, and so is the shore,
everything will still be,
for you and me
till there's no tomorrow to see.

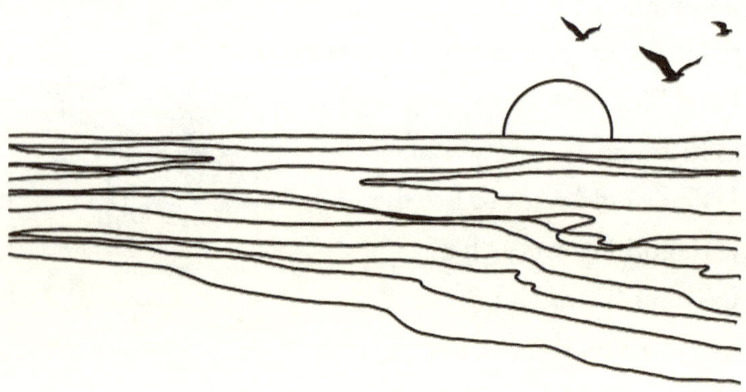

# Rest is rain

All beds grow cold someday—
In death, in despair, or heartbreak.
With ticking hearts and lamp-like eyes,
we lie, a maze of waiting, of staring into shadowed corners.
where past, present, and future blur;
falling softly, like rain.
Perhaps that's all everything becomes—rain.
The rest is rain.

# Bones and mud

Every time I hold him.
I feel nothing more than
a dead weight of bones and mud.
Hoping someday he will slide off me.
Evaporate, or stray away with the wind.
He lay there looking at me,
I see in him the remains of a war.
A soldier defeated by love.
Every loss stacked neatly on his back,
and he, slouching under the weight.
Asking me to snap this pain out of him,
but tell me, my dear,
How can I kiss you goodbye?
For I still hold the ashes.
of my beloved on my lips.
I've been here before,
I've been where you stand.
and I have asked too,
the way you ask.
I swallowed my words.

For, like stones, they fell on closed doors.
and made noise for the world to hate.
We all end here.
In someone else's arms,
begging them to carry our weight,
to take what we want to give.
Offer our souls like a whiff of perfume.
We all end here,
like a dead weight of bones and mud.

# A Curious child

You asked a question with no answer.
For the first time, I saw in you a child.
A child so curious
who dips his head
instead of his hand
for a taste that needs to be relished,
and not meant to be high on.

You didn't want to take your time.
I was meant to be read on nights most lonely,
days most bright, and thunders that kept you in.

I was not to be stretched.
Like a bedsheet on your soul.
But what more can I say about people?
whose hands are hungrier than their hearts.

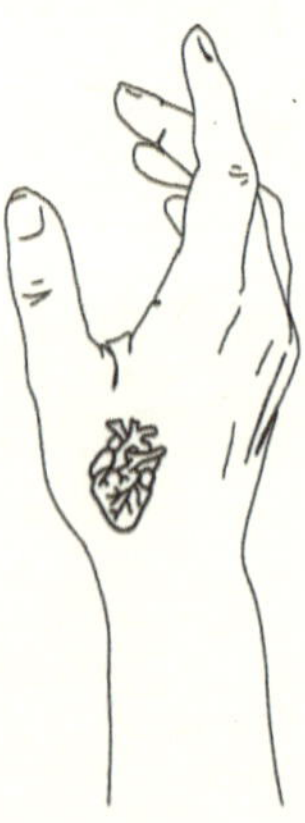

# *Reckless*

I can't tell you how many times
I've been dizzy,
by the vicissitudes of my love.
I spiral and reach the same bottom.
Every time, only to look up
and see your face,
pretending it's worthwhile.
Pulling your you, to my you,
in a licentious attempt,
to stop this spinning world.
and take a moment
for my dazed eyes to adjust to you.
My heart was in places
my head should have been,
reckless,
I offer my soul in the hands
that slip water and sand alike.

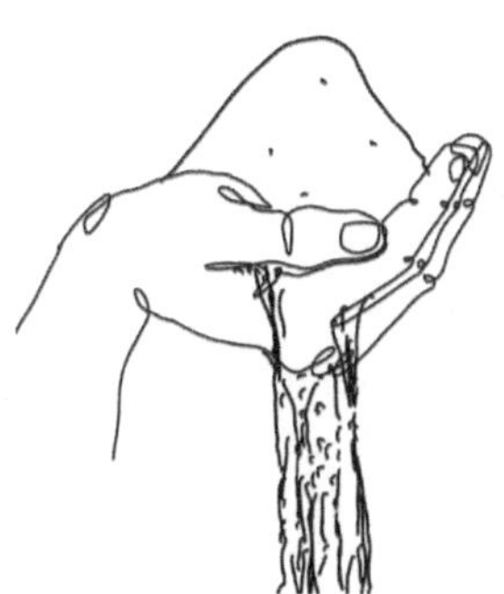
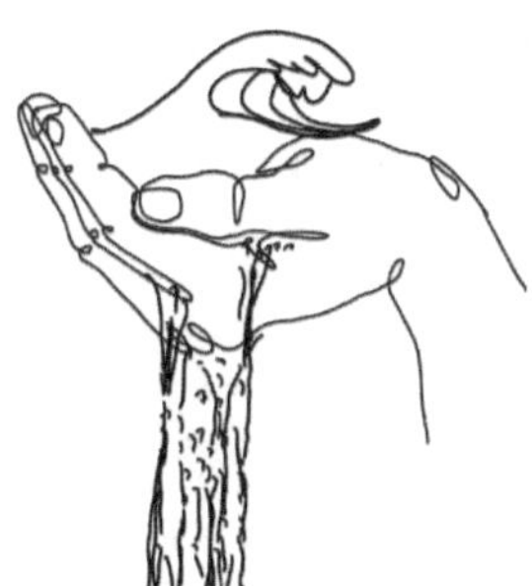

# *1 Iteration 2*

I stare into nothing,
and I hear nothing.
As I read a book, I stop mid-sentence,
and you pop up,
between one word and another.
Like a thought breaker,
I'm unable to move.
so consumed by you
running like a movie,
at the back of my head,
where I often take a seat
and everything outside,
seems just that, outside.
You've made a room in my head,
where I like to walk in,
in between two words,
two breaths,
two moments
and my carcass of a body.
just rifling and moving through the world.

To do things I have to do
and be things I have to be,
while completely living inside
Iterating and reiterating you.

# The Passerby

I met a man,
but he was not quite what he appeared to be.
He looked like a door,
not locked but not open either.
I walked in, regardless.
I admired the structure.
The pillars of strength,
the walls to keep solitude in,
the heart hidden under the carpet.
The good things they say,
are good in the same way,
but broken things
are never broken alike.
They are always unique, distinguished.
I found trinkets,
someone left behind, I thought.
A mug, a sketch, a candle, a vape.
I tucked them neatly.
I tried to dust the corners,
fix the windows,
hammer a nail to hang that crooked painting,
but nothing quite felt like it would stick.
I wandered the halls and sang songs,
but never to my heart's content.

A little hum and whisper here and there.

I watered the dead roots and sat in the darkness.

But nothing ever changed.

That is what you get,

for arriving at a place,

a little too early.

You become a passerby because it's not home yet.

# *I remain*

On a cold night, on an empty shore,
firewood stacked, flickering,
branches in a battle of ashes and fire;
A silent dance unfolding in your eyes.
Smoke whispers from your lips,
whiskey glass half buried, half surviving.
Did the shore, winds, or night compel your departure?
Or was it the silence within?

I watch as you leave,
eyes tracing your footsteps on the sand.
The leaf you crushed beneath,
I'm right there,
behind you,
where your heart hesitated.

In fading embers,
whiskey glass drifting to sea;
Each wave a slow farewell.
Smoke slips from your lips,
unnoticed by your gaze,
lost in the wind.

From my vantage,
I linger in your departing shadow.
We miss much in leaving,
Or perhaps stay for fleeting joy.
You craved beginnings,
I dwell in endings.

I remain,
in fading embers,
whiskey glass adrift,
and smoke trailing away,
lost in the wind.

I remain.
I was someone who watched the horizon,
long after the sun had set.
I was someone,
who remained.

# *I push, you pull*

The way I ran away from you,
was the way I was in love with you.
As desperate as the wave that travels to touch the shore;
as composed as the wave,
that eventually recedes.
Turning sand to silt,
drenching lovers in love
was what I did.

# Reeking of humans

I hate places that reek of humans.
In their bastardized versions of humanity,
the odor of their words and promises.
An abyss of dead dreams piling on one another.
The way expectations ooze from their eyes.
The stench of intentions.
I've gloved myself from people,
Those who flicked my forehead every time I tried to raise it.

## *2x2*

I leaned against the wall,
staring at the cracks,
imagining a 2x2 window.
I had stopped looking outward.
A quarter filled with pain,
another with regret,
one with a facade for others
and the rest cradled memories of you.
Days passed, just rocking in my chair.
I held some hands, left a few,
kissed a few lips, spat out a few.
You poisoned me, visibly,
veins once green now black.
I was fragile anew,
sun scorching, snow freezing,
each a metaphor of your pain,
trying to embody my existence.
I tore down doors and built walls,
ones that looked like yours back from the day you left.
The walls shivered
with a knock, a heartbeat—familiar.
You call, asking if I thought of you.

I did, unconsciously,
among blinking and heartbeats,
but I'll never unseal my lips,
to tell you what you've made of me.
I've made peace with it.
Now, in my chair, rocking,
syncing with each tick,
finding peace with my remnants,
second by second.

# *The Corner*

Everybody has a special place in their home,
that is really close to their heart.
Something that comforts,
cozy.
That makes home, feel like home.
Something that makes their heart
pound against their ribs.
Me? I have a place like that.
An empty corner.
I kept no furniture there.
It had far too many memories to be covered by furniture.
No, it was not a corner where my father
marked the walls with my height as I grew up.
It wasn't where I saw my grandma
knitting sweaters for winter.
No, it wasn't where I decorated my dollhouse.
That corner was a place where I fit in-
like a piece of a puzzle.
That corner was an altar that heard my honest prayers.
A tabernacle where I kept my weakest me.
Sometimes curled up,
holding my head between my bent knees.

A place that I was one with,
in body,
in emptiness,
in silence.
The corner was one I trusted.
It took many missed hits,
of the bat, of the belt, of the fist.
It was where I crawled up like a fetus
and prayed to travel back to my mother's womb.
And now, I still keep it empty.
Just in case there's another hand,
another bat, another belt.
Just in case.

# Uncovered

I stood there,

petrified at the way that wall stared at me.

There hung the most beautiful moments of us,

now just an empty wall,

with a hole and a nail stuck in it.

Uncovered only

by the last goodbye.

Just like your hand slipping away from mine—

uncovered,

here on my palm where I held you last,

I now see the hole and the nail stuck in it.

# *Sparks!*

We were like two pebbles,
chipping away at each other.
Losing fragments, breaking imperfectly
but we stayed.
We stayed for the sparks.
Oh, the sparks!

# Memory

There are a lot of things in this world I know
but far too little to show
I know the warmth of my father's pat,
I know the little corner ripped on his hat.
I know my mum's anklet sound.
Hiding a pink book, not to be found
I remember the petals from my boyfriend's gift.
The silent screams after the rift.
I remember my best friend rolling her eyes,
if another ever stole her fries.
I know the letters carved on the city park bench.
The whiskey I hated and the stench.
The pink fluffed frock I wore on my 6th birthday.
How everyone clapped and gave me way.
There are a lot of things in this world,
I remember and know
but far too little to surrender and show.

## *How is your relationship with your father?*

When asked, "How's your bond with your dad?"
My response is hesitant, never sad.
I know I'd cry if he left this life
but writing a eulogy would cut like a knife.
The pages would stay blank, not a word to say,
for our connection is neither dark nor day.
My father wasn't one to stray, but his presence never
seemed to stay.
We shared a home for twenty-six years,
yet he's a stranger, it appears.
Unlike my mother, whom I know so well,
My father's thoughts are a mystery, hard to tell.
What sparks his anger or calms his mind?
These are answers I cannot find.
Does he love me for who I've become?
Or does silence weigh what he wants to shun?
How do I find the middle ground where I grew?
Should I compare it to films or stories new?
But movies often stretch the truth,
and tales around me may lack the proof.
So, I settle for a word that's vague,
not too bright, not too grey.
"Okay" sums up the bond we share,

not too light, nor heavy to bear.
For I can't say for sure,
if I pack his temper in my little brain
or his hard work in my veins.
I can only say I have his button nose
and the brown of his skin,
that's where I end my resemblance to him.
So, when asked of my father, I simply say,
"Our bond is 'okay,'" and let it lay.

# *Circle*

I had a way of tearing pages
every time I wrote in love,
of people I once loved.
But you remained,
you had a way of coming back.
Like the impressions on the page after,
you had a way of reminding me,
what I let go with one hand.
and what I clutched tightly behind me in the other.
All I write now looks like
the scribbles of an angry child,
a straight line,
a slant,
a curve
and an immensely overlapped circle.

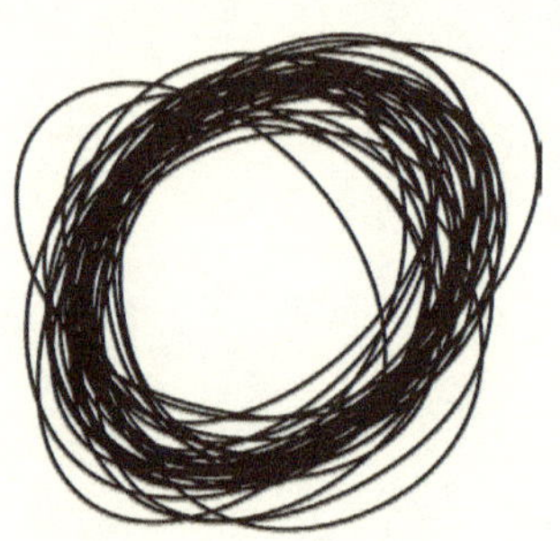

# A Mirror, Some Photographs, and Charms

# An empty day, week, month, year

The house echoes with silence.
The porch has waited endlessly.
The kitchen yearns for touch
and the sofa begs warmth on its empty seats.

In the light, there's just one shadow,
and in darkness, only one pair of footsteps.
On weekends, your wine glass clinks alone.
Your plate longs to harmonize with a pair of spoons.

The TV hums with brown noise,
void of conversation and laughter.
As you retire to bed,
creaky floorboards groan underfoot, battling the silence.

The bed recognizes your touch;
one side remains neatly tucked and cold.
You sink in, reminiscing about days and faces
now visible only behind closed eyes.

| MON | TUE | WED | THU | FRI | SAT | SUN |
|---|---|---|---|---|---|---|
|  |  |  |  |  |  | 1 |
| 2 | 3 | 4 | 5 | 6 | 7 | 8 |
| 9 | 10 | 11 | 12 | 13 | 14 | 15 |
| 16 | 17 | 18 | 19 | 20 | 21 | 22 |
| 23 | 24 | 25 | 26 | 27 | 28 | 29 |
| 30 |  |  |  |  |  |  |

# *Thunder*

They buried my voice
with layers and layers of mud.
They forgot
the brown of my skin was borrowed from the soil.

Sure, they couldn't hear me now,
but can they avert their eyes?
For I mothered a rose
with its roots deep in my veins
and a color bestowed by my heart.

Oh, the human folly—
you silence a voice
to witness the thunder.

# The Trader

I wish my mother instilled worth in me
and my father gave me the strength of his shoulders.

I wish my siblings taught me love,
And that I wasn't littered with the ruins of past lives.

I wish that everything I stand on weren't rocks
laid by my therapist,
And every band-aid wasn't borrowed from my friends.

As I stand here,
a beggar in the disguise of a merchant,
with empty hands,
trading love for love
is what I best taught myself.

# A half puzzle

Something doesn't fit,
like a puzzle with lost pieces.
Did you take it?
Did you take the pieces?

I ask every love that walks out the door,
No, put them back before you leave,
those are the rules.
But people can seldom put together.
what they break.
Maybe that is our biggest curse.

We are all loitering
in other people's lives
breaking things that don't belong to us
only to fix
what someone else broke within.

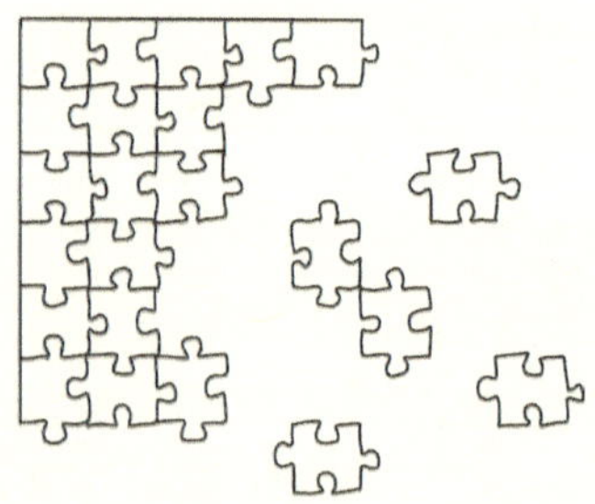

# Blood and Sweat

She carries the blood of a distant land;
Its warmth a memory, fading with each breath she takes.
Her sweat drips onto foreign soil;
building something she'll never own,
poured into hands that will never hold her roots.
The blood calls her home, but the sweat demands a future.
and neither side claims her fully—
She is a body divided,
belonging to neither past nor place;
A currency that never spends where it's owed.

# *Archives*

I don't want to do this anymore, I say.
I say this every dawn.
every dusk
everyday
"This"
and this is not the colorful problems
life keeps throwing at me
or that one job
I have put on hold for days
or that desk of mine
with papers on it
or the laundry
that's overflowing.
The "This" is
how deadly silent I feel inside.

Have you ever stared
into the quiet darkness.
With no clue of what's around?
The depth of the abyss inside
is 10 folds.

The "This" is how deafened by silence I am.

I wake up with
a taste of metal in my mouth.
and something
right in the center of my chest

churning my emotions 24/7.
How little everything has become in meaning
How I drag my insides to my body.
I may extend my hand and smile
when I see someone new.

Respond to mere Hello's and Hi's
like they are going to save my life.
But my soul curls up into a ball
at the sight of a new person.
Oh, the stench of decaying humanity.

This, I don't want to do this anymore.
Pretend like life around me
is actually seeping in through my skin.
It's not.
I'm long gone,
It's been years now
and I don't know
in which archives of myself I am to be found.
I'm long gone.

# *A virus*

You know how you feel when you're let go from the
hospital without being treated fully?
That is how I feel every day when I wake up.
Like the silent night, the sleep did nothing but just
pushed me into another day.
I walk around with untreated thoughts, slowly but
constantly picking at the scabs of the past.
Their self-hatred was so potent, it spread like sickness.
I wasn't immune to it,
I take shots of affirmations,
my soul is swallowing crystals.

My lungs are on the IV of scented oils and burning sage,
yet there's no cure for a restless heart.
Then someone yelled, "*Give it time.*"
So now I sync my heartbeats with the pendulum
Tick-tock, tick-tock.
Waiting for the hourglass to flip
and the stones piled up on my head to tumble down.

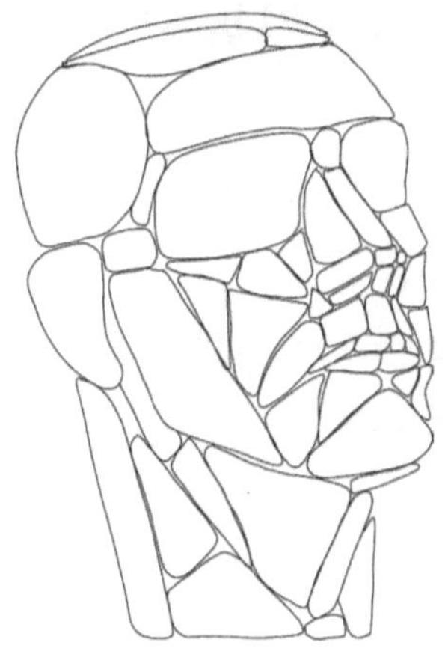

# *Sit*

They said sit still in one place until you can write exactly
how you feel
*I sat, I stared*
at the empty white wall before me,
and in that moment
I felt so alone
Would anyone ever know I lived?

I had no one
who knew exactly
which place in the city
makes me feel most like myself.
No person whose initials
I'd carve on a tree
I had no children
to carry on my legacy,
of dreamy eyes
and the way I bite the corner of my lips
when I focus too hard.
No one who knows my trivialities,
favorite color or food
or how I put the z in 'buzy'

In this room, as I sat and stared.
I felt what corpses must feel,
after their funeral.
When the last handful of soil,
is tossed over the casket
and people walk away.
You just lay there, no voice, no soul.
Feeling footsteps depart.

# *Paralysis of the human heart*

A condition.
To know what it wants
and to know it will never reach for it.
Like a painting of the Sistine,
A hypothetical hypocrisy.
Is it living in a paradox of dichotomy?
Repeatedly splitting the distance
between realization and acceptance.

Paralysis of the human heart,
like mistletoe of stones hung in your chest,
you sink, you drown in the noise,
unsure if the voices are within or apart.

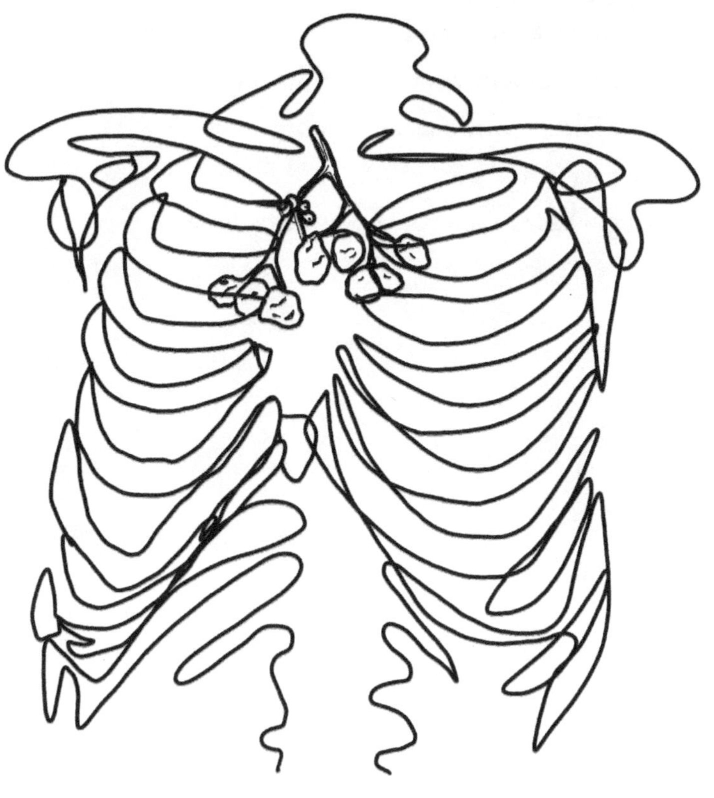

## *I wish I could tell you*

How I lull myself to sleep each night,
dipping my pen in the ink of my heart.
Writing poems that capture your essence.
Trying to lock you in my words to set myself free.
I like to pretend it was never about you,
yet I revisit the confines of memory,
wandering in and out,
burying what remains of you, little by little.

# *A prayer, a chant and an idol*

I wipe the blood from my wounds,
apply layers to conceal the scars.
My body, now the aftermath of your disaster.
I searched for love in every piece of myself I picked up,
every shard from when you shattered me,
chanting "I love you" over and over,
as if you knew it was a prayer striking my body,
returning each time, unaccepted.
You offered bruises as flowers,
saved my tears as your temple oil.
And now you come, kneel—not in prayer,
not in love, but in penance of lust, assuming you're forgiven.
I sit there with your head in my lap,
wondering how much say a stone has
in how it's loved

# A *puppets song*

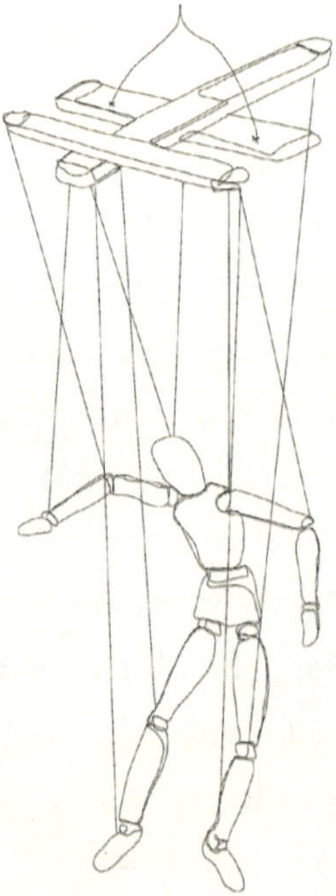

I kept banging on the walls,
until my fists were bloodied,
begging to be freed.
I sent screams to my mouth,
but my lips remained sealed,
an echo trapped within,
bouncing from my soul to my soul.
I sent anger to my head,
but it found its way to my eyes
I was trapped,
caught between head and heart,
entwining them in chaos.
I longed to break free,
to regain control over myself,
but only to smear my temple
with the ashes of those who burned me down.
Here I am, helpless,
watching this puppet-like body
force a smile.

## *How?*

Every time I see you, I wonder,
how did you forgive yourself while I still walked around,
carrying the weight of what you did to me?
Hung by me, in rags, tattered,
drenched in my tears, dripping my soul bit by bit.
Every time you smile at me, I want the earth to shake and
echo,
how did guilt walk itself out of you?
When I am the living reminder of how your demons,
feasted on me, smacking their lips;
watching me in pain.
How?

# Sunflowers

The sunflowers in my village had curved spines.
They were always taught
that facing the earth made them more modest
than lifting their heads up and following the sun.

# The mantel piece

Throughout my life,
I've likened myself to the ocean,
only to realize my tides
were mere jolts in a bottle,
carefully placed on a child's mantel,
as they playfully rocked it,
sending ripples through my existence.

Perhaps that's the nature of life,
one person's world is another's souvenir.

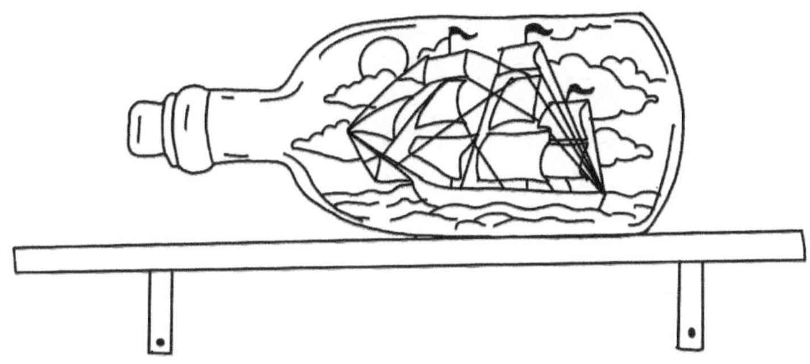

# *Stripped*

Navigating through life like a wildflower
through huge castle walls,
unaware of the height ahead,
paving through cold bricks.
It's difficult here, you know,
when you hear your voice rarely,
and the only one you hear is you
talking to yourself from within,
echoing through your system,
almost vibrating like a guitar string
through and through, you.
Have you lived and really lived?
Can you feel those moments
like they destroyed you yesterday?
Like a hug that forever remained in your arms,
like a past crossroad you walk by every day,
afraid to make a decision.
And you carry these on you forever—
sometimes, like the pearls you're so proud of,
and sometimes like the neatly hidden greys in your hair.
These moments, gone, passed and buried,
define so much for you.
They become the sight of your brain
and the walk of your heart.

Treading lightly through all of these,
tiptoeing through a tear mine,
wondering if there ever would be
gay pastures ahead
where you just walk again
with all this stripped from you.

## *Against all reality*

Like piercing screams,
from a mouth glued tight.
A heart wandering left,
against all reasons right.
Like a palm soaked in blood
swiped across my tender lips,
monstrosity of a puppet play
life so often mimics.
Like words scattered apart
before a hungry literate,
licking his way to a poem,
like fire, his tongue be lit.
Let this be written down
by veins of desperation,
a part of me forever stationed.
There's a world beneath my skin,
as real as I have always been,
turning myself inside out,
'cause I want you to see.
There's a world in me against all reality.

# *A moth to fire*

It was pain in people that attracted me, like moth to fire.
burned and bruised, I would still flutter around for more.
Pain, like flowers growing on your back
through every little crevice, every little crack
and when I hold you, these flowers of yours rub on me
like little specks of fire, burning and bruising, I would still
come back for more.
Pain, like an ocean clashing within a mass of bones and
blood.
I was never one to dip a toe and run back to the shore.
I walked deep and held my breath a little too long.

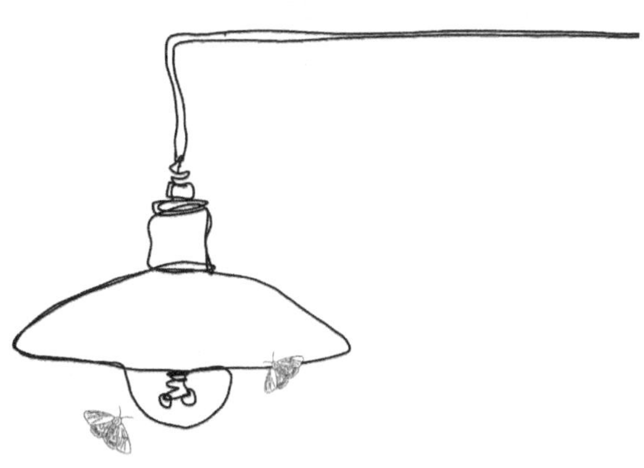

# The past is a narrative

Museums, like time preserved in little bottles
pots and pans
telling stories that begin with *"probably"* and *"maybe"*...
that is the best part, you don't know,
no one knows, how time decays in its ashes
the memories that once lived.
We wander around the earth
as mere spectators of these stories,
to one day leave our own inaccurate past,
that would stumble from someone else's lips
and begin with a *probably* and *maybe*.

# *I'll never know*

I am one of those few people who will never know
what it is like to be loved unconditionally.
I won't know what it feels like,
when someone chooses you every day.
I'm one of those who put their love up on curbs
for someone to grab it and call it theirs.
and still at the end of the day, the week, or the month
grab it all back again, because it was left there untouched.
I fear being one of those messenger bottles,
God threw in the ocean of the world;
never to be found by anyone, never to be read.
And no, I am not being pessimistic,
maybe some destinies, some lives are meant to be lived
this way
to humanize pain, for sadness to live in, for loneliness to
have a face.
This is where it survives; this is where they live,
in people like me, and maybe this is their destiny I get to
fulfil.
So generations would know that pain can be beautiful
and sadness can survive the day.

# Till death do us part


I heard people say this to one another,
Oh, how romantic, I thought!
Later as I grew up, I heard it with new ears
Death do us part, they say,
Was it a disclaimer? Was it a loophole?
I wondered what else could I escape from, with this
"promise"?
Till death do us part!
Can I say that to every yes I said, when I meant a no?
Can I say that to the rock tied to my heart,
or the lump in my throat?
Can I say that to these shaking hands and tears that roll?
Can I say that to the fear, the doubt,
and despair of the soul?
Please, oh God, please!
May death do us part.
To each one of them, I say,
*"Till death do us part."*

# How to mourn the one who isn't dead

How to mourn the one who isn't dead?
They're gone and they're never coming back.
Alive, living their life but dead in yours.
How do you mourn the one who isn't dead?
When their name tastes like blood in your mouth,
the disrespect pounding on your eardrums,
Their presence now only clothes forgotten in the closet.
Their conscious choice, a visitor on the front porch you
don't address.
You, love, are alive too, but forgotten.
For memory, you see, is a cracked jar.
and sometimes when people forget who you are,
it gets easier to be who you are.

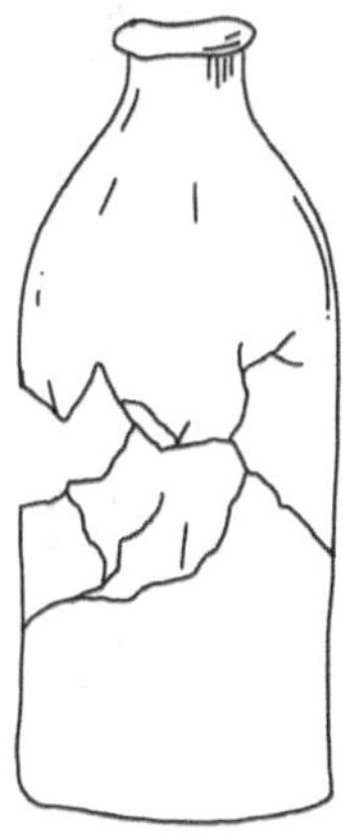

# *Unabandoned*

That's the way it is, my dear,
You won't be abandoned
You will stay with yourself
Your demons, your saints
your good deeds and bad.
*All*
It's a boon and a curse.
to be abandoned by people
is how life goes, but
to be abandoned by oneself
is how death creeps into your soul
It is what you must fear.

# Beyond the Milky Way

It is beyond the Milky Way.
and it's within your soul.
We must think we have something in common
with the universe,
even if it is only darkness.

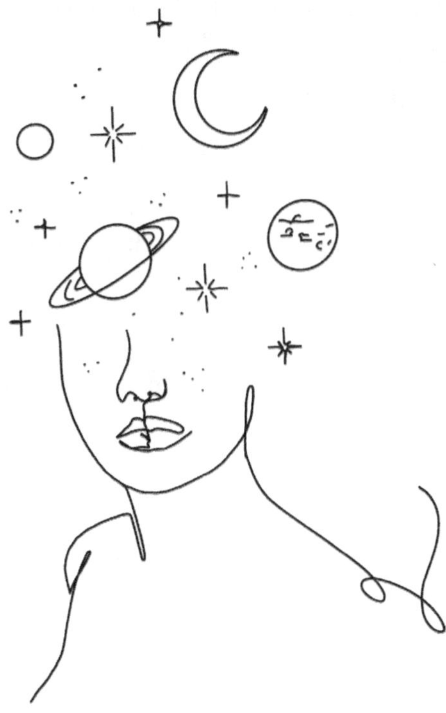

# I've always been on a boat

I've always been on a boat
drifting,
sometimes I grab the tiller
and pivot to the room my body is in.
I try to drop the anchor,
let my feet reach the abyssal and form roots,
but I'm a sailor.
I've barely lived in the now.
more often than not, I've lived in the past
and I've lived in the future,
while completely only breathing in the present.
The boat is still.
The waters are still.
The anchor lies there at the bottom of the ocean.
still.
Stillness, of the vessel,
is rarely stillness of the soul.

# *What if death is not a tall man*

What if death is not a tall man
in a black cloak?
What if it comes in the face of a lover?
Would we then ease into its arms?
feed on its voice
and curl up into its lap?
What if death comes with all the possibilities
that life does?
What if death is indeed not the end
but the beginning?

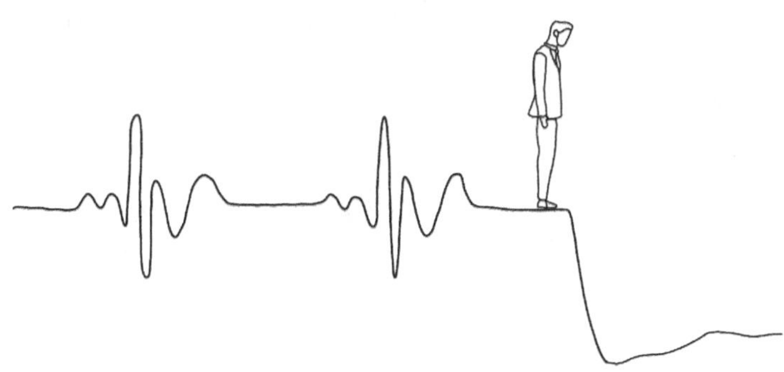

# Where does love come from?

Where does love come from?
Is it from the ease you never felt?
All the grief you ever dealt?
Where does love come from?
Is it from the need
Or is it from the want?
Where does love come from?
A thought of thought,
does it come from the need of giving,
what you never got?
Where does love come from?

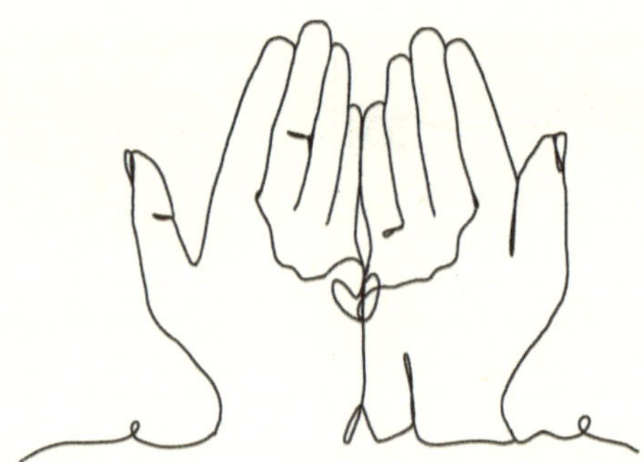

# Wildfire

With my whole world burning within me,
I wanted to be a wildfire,
burn those who came with torches,
and called it love.

# Lost and if found

I lost parts of me,
like misplacing things in my room—
an earring lost with my patience;
A lip gloss, with my voice,
A bookmark, with my words.
I know I will find them,
days, months, or weeks later.
When I do, I'll cry,
and tell them how much I missed them,
placing each safely back where it belongs.

# *Hell is a playground*

While you came with your pitchforks and sticks,
trying to push me off,
I sat at the edge of the cliff,
ready to sink to the bottom of the sea,
with my sins tied around my neck.
You stole my solitude
and my last confession before death.
You ensured I lived and died in hell.

# Grass on the other side

Love came to me, but life's plan turned it into longing.
Love came to me like a phantom limb,
present but physically absent,
A wound that won't heal,
A persistent ache to which time is no medicine.
love came to me,
Like a locked door with no key,
I forever wonder what is on the other side.
or a kite without wind;
Yearning to soar but bound to stillness.
love came to me,
Like an unfinished song,
the melody lingers, but I can't find the words.
It came to me like an echo in the canyon,
reverberating and returning without fulfilment.
Love came to me like a beautiful garden,
But it was always winter.

# Reverse déjà vu

Some people, places, and parts
of our life, leave.
They walk backwards,
Like a reverse déjà vu,
A reality that steps back,
into a dream you can't quite remember.

# What did you become out of sight?

The women who held back their words,
With anger clenched in fists, unheard,
counted miles they couldn't tread;
or shades they couldn't wear instead,
Dreams left on pillows in the night,
What did you become out of sight?

Did you become gentle and meek?
Polite whispers when you speak?
A traveler within four walls confined?
Or a shade where you are hard to find?
Or did you flip that pillow to weep?
A graveyard of dreams buried deep?

Convenient women fade from view,

neither present nor shaping what's new.

Say those words, don't hold them back,

throw hands when under attack;

Move countries, wear that red,

Tie your dreams upon your head.

Silly? Who cares? Stand and fight,

For being beautiful, kind and polite,

are owned, not paid for in cost,

Fierce, loud, opinionated are virtues never lost.

# *Survival*

My feet were always cold,
maybe they were telling me to run.
Run away from everything,
or stay and step on today's burning coals.
The rest of my body disagreed;
A hearth in my chest healed my heart like a ceramic bowl.
Strong enough to hold everything, yet still brittle.
They say the body carries emotions.
It bears everything you feel.
What I felt, and when I felt it,
was like a sauna and a cold plunge.
My feelings kept me on edge,
half rejected, half accepted,
maintaining a temperature for survival.

# A Light Through the Cracks and Some Keys

## *100 ways*

Every shattered mirror on the ground
still reflects the sky.
This time not in one,
but in a hundred different pieces,
in a hundred different ways.

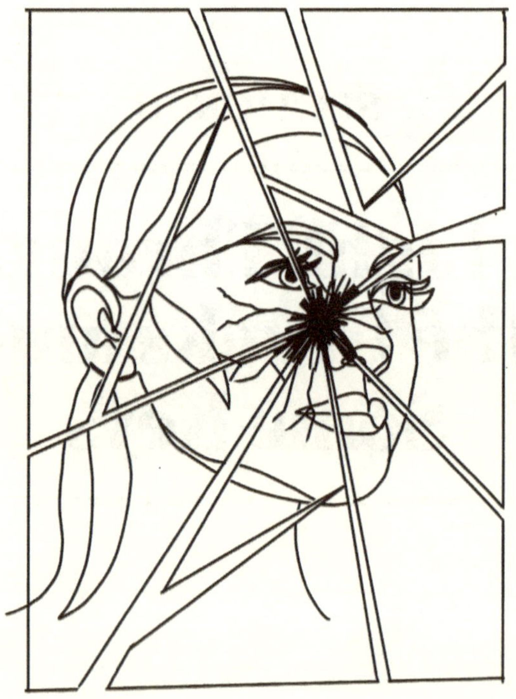

Every shattered mirror on the ground

# Of tranquility

I'm no longer a tidal wave,
nor a tranquil lake.
I've weathered extremes;
from shouting at the world around me
to tearing at my own heart.
Now, I sit beside the river,
skipping stones to the rhythmic pulse.
This solitary moment is precious,
where nothing else matters,
I would not care if everything else fell off this earth.

## Even it out

I liked to keep myself airtight,
sealed all my cuts and scars.
Until, one morning I saw the sun break through the
clouds.
Every ray fell freely until it pierced the ground and
swallowed it whole.
I opened my bandages one by one,
Letting my light out.
I let the sun within me, rise.
As the night now lay with my shadows,
falling behind me.
The dark mistress of the absent moon was defeated; my
purpose there was done.
I wore her on my shoulders like a cape,
falling behind, dragging with every step I took.
I parted my lips, letting the light out,
opened my mouth to a full roar.
The world will witness the aftermath of our collisions.
Destruction.
Let me see if this time we can create a better world.
A better breed of human-faced animals.
After all this,

I'll carry the light on my face,
and the darkness on my back,
And this time, in this way,
we will even the world out.

# Tell Me You Will Survive

When the storm rips through your soul
and the winds howl like wolves at your door.
When the earth shifts beneath you,
turning your every step into a battle with gravity—

Tell me you will survive.

When the night crushes you under its weight
and silence becomes a river, pulling you under.
When hope feels like a forgotten dream,
a distant star burned out long ago—

Tell me you will survive.

You are not the broken branch,
snapped by the first gust of wind.
You are the oak that stands after the fire,
roots deep, unyielding, the storm reduced to whispers.

Tell me you will survive and I'll believe it too.
In my prayers, I'll bookmark your name
and whisper into the ears of Gods
a wish for your victory.

And when you tell me you survived,
I'll turn the page and this time pray that you live too.

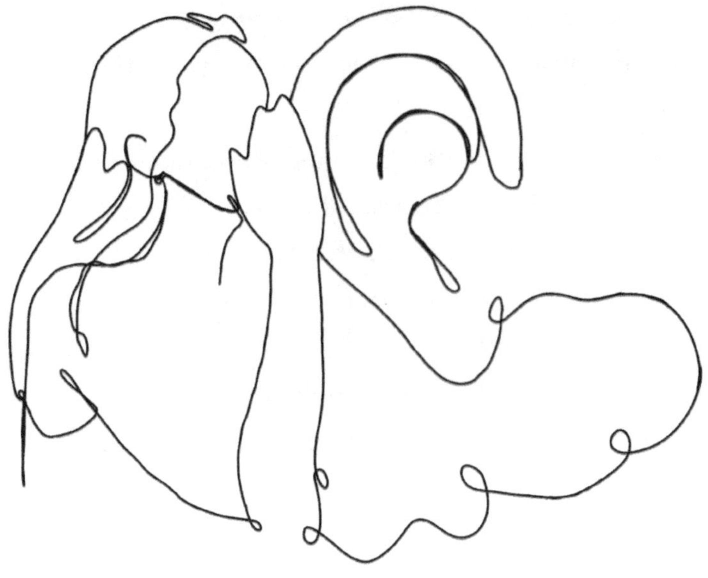

## *Head up, Shield down.*

Sometimes good things don't just happen.
They need to be received.
They could be standing right at the edge of the line you drew,
guarding yourself from the world beyond.
Lay down that shield. Step out into the light.
Imagine the warmth of the sun on your face,
The soft whisper of possibilities beckons you forward.
That one good thing—
could be a sunrise breaking through the storm,
a whisper of kindness in a sea of noise,
a touch of hope in the midst of doubt.
It could be one of the best things
that happens to you.
Open your heart like a child's embrace
and witness the unexpected lift you up.

# Circle of existence

We all have a circle,
a circle containing
the past, the future, the being,
not being, the lies, and most importantly, the truth.
We circle the circumference.
Some, striving for the center, others drifting.
Some unaware, some indifferent.
Our lives are spent walking, running and swimming along
the radius.
Yet, we're constantly drawn back to the shores of illusion.
An illusion of existence,
distant from your own version of it.
The shore offers temporary relief
but binds you,
preventing you from discovering your true ocean.
I long for that ocean—
an expanse of truth in its rawest form.
Reflecting my essence,
revealing all I can become.
Guide me away from these chains,
the constraints of the shore.
For I belong to the primal sea,
the one from which I emerged;
In the depth of my mother's womb—
A boundless ocean of self.

# The chase

They will chase you,
Like you're a butterfly in the garden.
Stretch out their arms and run after you,
making you feel desirable, vulnerable.
One that would fit perfectly in their palms
and leave a beautiful nebula dye on their fingertips,
once they're done ripping your wings off.

Preserve them in pages of books long lost
and stacked on their shelves.

When they do this, remind them,
You're an eagle or a vulture, even.
You soar the sky, high above and their stretched-out arms
fall short.
Their sight too weak to spot you.

Know you're desirable,
know they're vulnerable.

# *Miles and miles.*

And I walked, miles and miles and miles, looking for her.
When she was buried miles and miles within.
Digging her out only a handful at a time,
for this world does not believe,
in the dead coming to life,

So she lays there,
like a Bible without God in it.
Prayers without an Amen.

She is the prologue engraved on a mossy tombstone but
I assure her that when she rises,
we will walk miles and miles and miles, together,
being who we are meant to be.

For the past, the present and the future
 can be wrapped and tucked
at frail edges neatly into one person.

We will walk miles and miles and miles
 never to be buried again.

# The exit sign

Every time I thought I found love,
I also learned how to get over it,
Every beginning comes with an end, they say
and every person I met made me better at how to get over
them, more than how to love them,
Every person became a 12- point article on how to move on.
and in every person I found and knew, I searched for the
exit sign,
Because I knew one day I had to walk out through it.
and eventually, it became more about finding the exit sign,
Walking through it and reveling in the aftermath of a loss
I chose.
Every person is like a portal I walked through,
Every person has a horizon on which my angels and
demons zip-lined,
until one tipped the other over.
But now, I'll stay.
I'll learn how to enter a door and not go looking for the exit.
to jump in the pool and not panic when my feet can't find
the floor.
and I'll blink on their faults like they blink on mine,
and not blindfold my way out.

I hope this time when I find love,
it is worthy of me being the one who stays
and I no longer run the race to the end.
Alone, again, in haste.

## *My Frilly Socks*

I loved my frilly socks,
my favorite childhood accessory.
I wore them everywhere: to the playground, to church
and Sunday school.
They were little parachutes for my feet,
telling me I could tip-tap-toe anywhere
and dip-dap-do anything.

But then, I grew up and stopped wearing them altogether.
A few years passed, and my feet, once meant to fly,
had somehow grown roots into the world.

But the world has now shifted.
I've heard the frilly socks are back,
and made for adults too.
I guess everyone simultaneously realized
that we rooted our feet instead of our heart.
We're still allowed to sail the sky.
The frilly socks are yours if you dare to put them on
again.
Those little parachutes for the feet,
sailing the travelers away!

# *I want to fall asleep*

I yearn to see you again
but this time in a cozy corner of a broken castle.
Warming ourselves by the fireplace
wrapped in one another
on a bed of white linen.
With daisies growing from the cracks in the floor
and creepers on the walls,
where the only sound is that of the ambers burning.
Bit by bit, moment by moment,
with rain pattering outside.

I want to fall asleep
Just the way I fell in love.

Slowly, letting my senses go one at a time
feeling safe.
And when I wake up to still see your face smiling back at
me.

# Break free

Everything in life doesn't come in pairs.
Everything cannot be repaired.
Everything unbroken is unbroken the same way
but what breaks, breaks differently, they say.

So, if you must break,
I hope you break like the clouds and gift rain.
May you break like a seed and grow grain.
May you break like a fast that cleanses the sin
or a glass at a Greek wedding.
May you break like the first ray of dawn,
leaves, flowers, and life to spawn.

May all your breaking with a purpose and beauty be.
May you break if needed to *break free*.

# *Oh to be human!*

I often think of how I could be anything
but I was blessed with a human life.
How generations cascade from womb to womb
and see the world a little differently each time.
How we come home and share our day,
like a mere exchange of reading glasses
and hope they see and feel what we say.
How love sticks like pollen on the back of a bee
travels from person to person,
budding a story.

Oh! to be human.
Like sandcastles pretending to be the Rockies.
We are made with too much detail,
color of the soil, eyes of the ocean, veins like vines,
the darkness in our ribs, like the darkness of space.

Oh! to be human.

Living in the twilight of themselves,

half asleep, half awake.

We mumble wishes at the port of faith

and our little hearts like lighthouses;

blink

and hope our prayers find their way.

# *The critic*

I see the world through a magnifying glass,
catching what slips beneath the surface—
The way sunlight fractures, through a water glass
and paints a fleeting mosaic on the table.
How the wind presses a leaf to the ground,
Its veins, visible, like a map abandoned.
The faint hesitation in someone's voice
before they say, "I'm fine".
The threadbare patience in a mother's gaze
as her child pulls at her hem.

I collect these fragments,
turn them over like coins,
weigh their worth.
Wonder why others pass them by.

A crack in a polished marble floor
tells me a story of its making.
An untouched cup of coffee
is a monument to a distracted mind.
But perhaps I look too hard,
peel too much away,
criticize the quiet,
just to give it a name.

Ah, but why does it matter?
What is my gaze to anyone?
Eyes of a hundred admirers
feed the fire of creation,
but the solitary eye of a critic—
mine or another's—
sharpens the blade of purpose.

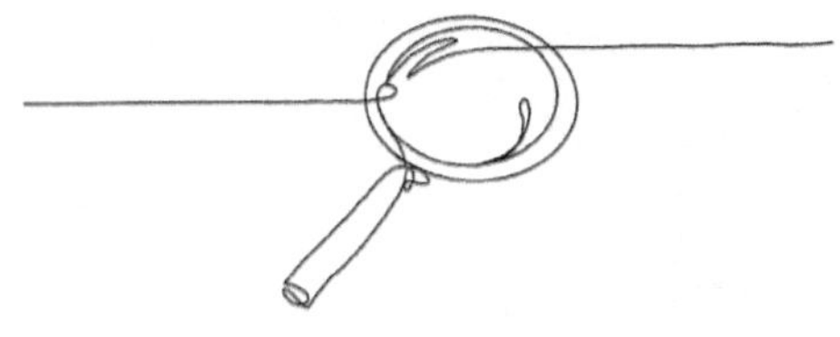

## *What experience does?*
## *Differentiates.*

Often with all the roses that pricked our fingers,
we are forced to accept deserts as our fate.
But, remember
that if you live in a desert
long enough,
even dandelions look like sunflowers.
Devoid of beauty,
moss on the wall looks like art
and
devoid of company for long enough,
thieves look like knights.

# *Makes sense?*

To wake up into the coffee and drink your morning,
to take a grass on that walk.
Pick a smell and flower it.
To turn your nights off and crawl into the lamp.
It's perfectly okay to make no sense
*When the sense around you makes no world.*

# Tilted

You see, how the horizon is tilted?
maybe it's a sign,
that I too am a tilted line
and somewhere your horizon is a little tilted too.
I wonder if they'd ever meet.
Or is it possible only if we are on different Earths?
I know, I wouldn't wait and jump from mine to yours,
to find that field beyond right and wrong that Rumi
promised,
where lovers meet.

# *A take on kindness*

Kindness is a form of love

It's the one that exudes what you have in you.

It's how you speak, when you're hurt

It's how you show up for yourself and others.

Kindness is faith in the fact that all things have a purpose.

*When you recognize the purpose, it's impossible to not be kind.*

# *Would you ever hear the beep?*

You wake up in the morning,
brew your first cup of coffee.
But then, a parcel is delivered.
The coffee machine beeps, telling you it's done.
You ignore it and take care of the delivery.

You get back, but then your laptop beeped
So you tend to that,
while eyeing a basket of laundry in the bin.
So you go and put it in the washer.

You reheat your coffee in the microwave
and then comes a task,
and another,
The microwave beeps,
but then again there's a task
and another.

How many times, my love, have you done that to yourself?
Let the world drown out what you needed?
Like a wishbone between you and the world, and
somehow in the tug,
the world always gets the bigger piece.

For once now, take that cup,
filled with the sweet nectar of wants and needs,
swirling in your heart, and
let the world be where it belongs.

It can wait.

# A *morning's promise*

The sun lifts itself over the horizon,
effortless, steady—
With a warmth I cannot muster.
Birds spill songs into the air,
sharp and clear,
while my voice chokes.
on the edges of unsaid things.

The trees sway with the wind,
each movement so graceful,
while I stumble through my steps,
unsure where I am meant to go.

By the end of the day,
I notice everything—the quiet resilience
of flowers leaning into the light;
The river's easy way of moving forward.

And I think,
I could have done better,
should have been softer,
stronger,
or more sure of myself.

Still, the horizon shifts again.
Another morning awaits,
Its promise steady as the sun.
Maybe tomorrow,
I'll find the rhythm
That seems so natural
to everything else.

## *Walking away*

Their backs speak louder than faces—
A silent symphony of abandonment,
where ribs become arches
of homes they built
and shoulders sag with the weight
of stories, they weren't meant to carry.

Books and canvases know this pose too well;
A woman walking away.
Her spine stretched taut like a thread
pulled between worlds—
One unravelling behind her,
another stitching itself ahead.

"I hugged places that unmade me,
Let people seep into my skin
like spilled ink.
Now, look at my back—
It holds every scar, every ghost,
a map of what I survived."

Is the strength in the leaving?
Or in the journey to somewhere unnamed?
Maybe her turned back is no retreat,
but the budding of wings.

Somehow, I am curious
to see the faces of these women
photographed, painted, sketched walking away.
I want to see what hope looks like,
etched on the faces
of women who dare to step into the unknown.

# Carried by light

Each kept promise lingers,
a thread of light stitching the torn edges of the world.
Each kind word roots itself like a seed,
sprouting warmth in the coldest places.
Every gentle touch of reassurance
becomes a torch passed hand to hand.

The more these moments bloom,
The brighter the world becomes—
A constellation of quiet radiance,
pushing back against the void,
filling even the hollowest corners
with a possibility of dawn.

This light is ours to tend.
It grows with every choice to care,
every act of love,
until one day,
It is enough to set the earth
spinning in its glow.

# *Light catcher*

I plan to hang a light-catcher on my eyes
whenever I see the end of the tunnel.
Let the hope scatter through my soul.
So, the next time I'm lost within myself,
I know that all I have to really do, is open my eyes.

# Is it a coffee or a whiskey day?

May your passionate bodies grow old and wise,
and may Love become the staff on which you rise.
When your eyes are too weak to see,
may Love remind you how beautiful it all can be.
When hope seems to fizzle and fade away,
may love be the warm hands that say –
words so many with a gentle touch,
May love fill your vase and mean so much.

Pull the curtains when the light's too bright,
May love polish your glasses and make things right.
May love sit beside you and gently ask,
"What's wrong?" and help with every task.
May love fill you up, overflow your skin,
and when all is done, through thick and thin,
may love, stand by and softly say,
*"Is it a coffee or a whiskey day?"*

# Pain

Pain will not slip through your fingers like water
It will rise like tides
through your bloodstream.
It will stay like a splinter in your heart.
Pain
Demands to be loved, before it can be released.
It's like a crying child; you hug gently.
Sit your pain in a chair,
hold its hand and ask it,
Where does it hurt?
Let its quiet sobbing whispers guide you.
Then, when you understand it,
Ask it to open its fist and let it go.

# *How many, how much?*

How many waves in a shallow lake?
How many days does a ghost wake?
How many religions does an atheist know?
How many afternoons burn mellow?
How many excuses can a believer make?
How many truths can a liar stake?
How much faith can a skeptic show?
How much love can a beggar borrow?
How many sins does a priest confess?
How many heads does a sinner bless?
How many deaths does one life take?
How many iterations does a circle make?
How many? How much?
She said as many, as much.
For life has demons, yours and mine. Take as many, as
much for you to shine.

# Looking forward to.

If God didn't make death,
time would be an endless stretch, waiting would have no
meaning.
Pain would last an eternity,
and would poison then be a medicine?
If God didn't make death,
there would be no end to human suffering.
Breath wouldn't find release, hearts caged in endless time,
My will wouldn't see the light of day.

Thank God for death,
for I know, everything will end.
Sooner or later, my body will get lighter,
releasing the mountain of a soul
it gets crushed every day.
Thank God for death, for in that anticipation,
I have something to look forward to.

# The photograph

Years later, I saw it,
'the photograph'
Like a party trick concealed the truth.
I, like the audience,
captivated by the beauty of lies.

Lies, I thought in an instant. Are they all that bad?
Some lies bring comfort
and for years I sat in its cosy lap, watching them weave me
a blanket
Oh! the photograph.
A time when nothing seemed impossible.
One day I'll shine so bright, I'll swallow the sun.
Lick the nectar of a volcano running off my hands.
Sprint as far as I can,
trampling a meadow of stars under my feet.

On the contrary, the sun was always in eclipse, so I didn't
get started on the rest.

And all the photos after that didn't quite have the same
smile.
"What happened?"
I'd expect you to ask.
"I don't quite remember."
I tried to pinpoint an incident.

Like throwing darts at a whiteboard,
everything a bull's-eye, everything a miss
But my life, as I know it, is in two parts:
before the photograph and after it.
Our stories, though different, all have,
'A *photograph moment*'
and a before,
and an after.

## *One question*

Such is the curiosity of a simple human heart,
if I could fit every single question,
every wonder,
every doubt in this world into one line,
it would only echo an infinite series of
Why?

Such is the curiosity of a simple human heart.

# *North Atlantic*

I swam the
North Atlantic
the other day,
In thirty minutes, life became clear.
Don't linger where the waves break;
step in - less shallow, more sincere.
When a wave comes crashing down, don't struggle,
don't resist its flow.
In the overwhelm, stay still, for sometimes, peace is
letting go.
With every tide you'll rise anew, stronger with the storms
you've been through!

# *A map of whos.*

They asked,
"How long ago did you lose yourself?"
But I heard,
"How long ago would we have lost you?"
21 years ago.
9 years ago.
5 years ago.
Two nights ago.
Had I succeeded.

I still don't know what kept me tethered.
What gripped me so tightly at the edge of that cliff, not to
pull me back up—
But to keep me hanging there, dangling.
I wasn't fighting to rise;
I was fighting to cut loose.

I am a tattered paper—
not with details of where or how I fell, but a badly
scribbled map of
WHO
happened to me.
Names, faces, fragments of a life I didn't choose.
The sunrises from where I swayed were golden; the
sunsets like dreams.

The birds, the valleys - untouched, perfect.
But beneath it all, I could smell it—
the world, rotting, decaying,
just like me.
The nature in me was pure, pristine.
But the nurture, was a slow bleed of innocence.
Cut me loose, so I can return, and this time,
Maybe - just maybe - I'll make it better.

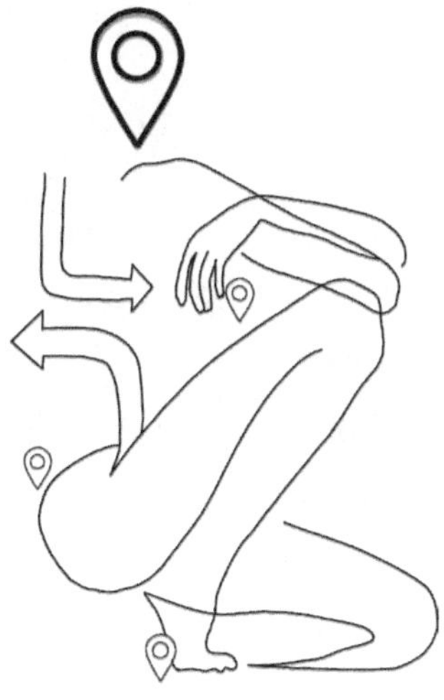

# *Without*

As I grew older, I realized there's no such thing as
'without'
I knew that the moment someone said,
"Oh, I can't - not without you."
Without?
Once a person enters your life, you're never truly without
them.

Memories don't orphan people the way people do;

They cling to you like soft drapes of your soul
or wrap around you like sunlight on a warm day.
The life we live together,
isn't just a cascade of breaths we take to survive.
It's a spark from a firecracker in the sky,
a brief shimmer that descends all around us.
We choose which lights to look at,
and those become our story.
So no, there is no *without*.
Something within me will forever hold a piece of every
person I've met,
like gravity holding the Earth together.

# The fire is hungry

It starts in the pit of my stomach.
Sometimes it burns my lungs to ashes.
At times, it also crowns my head.
in mighty upward flames.
I notice it often sizzling at my bare feet,
and sometimes I've noticed it melting my neck like glass,
when I bow before the unseen.
I've seen it in my gaze,
like sparks of words unsaid.
I've also seen it spread like wildfire
down every section of my spine.
The heart tossed in the hearth of this body,
It's a baptism by fire of demons in its inferno.
This time around,
the fire is hungry.

### *Hey, you've reached Monica, I can't come to the phone right now.*

I am busy writing melancholic poems,
finishing a painting, I started 6 months ago,
picking up the pack of pencils fallen
at the back of my bed,
watering plants and praying they survive;
learning the language of musical notes.
I'm at the library flirting with books of the season.
I can't come to the phone right now
because I know I once held the ocean in my heart.

Look, the moon is out.
I'm sorry I can't come to the phone tonight.
It's high tide; I must rise.

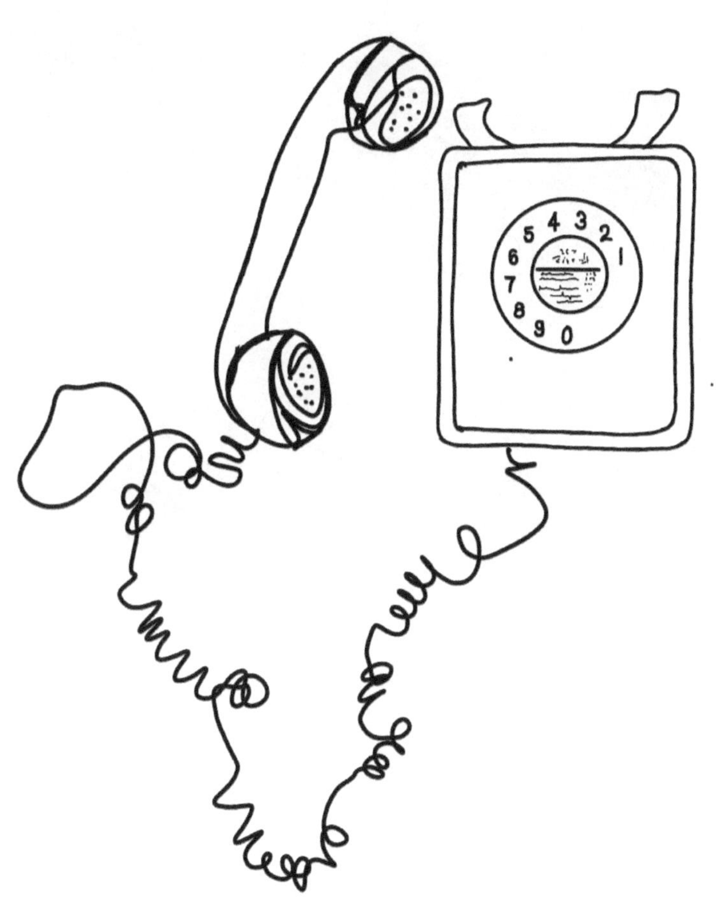

# *Acknowledgments*

To those who filled my attic with memories and lessons, whether joyful or painful. To my readers, thank you for wandering through these pages with me.

A special thank you to Akanksha Sanjay Rai for your creative vision and the inspiration you brought to the illustrations. Your ideas shaped the visual journey that accompanies these poems, and I'm deeply grateful for your collaboration.

To my sister, for pushing me to take the leap and publish this book. Your encouragement and belief in me were the spark I needed to bring this dream to life.

www.ingramcontent.com/pod-product-compliance
Lightning Source LLC
Chambersburg PA
CBHW022011150726
47990CB00002B/603